IN MEMORY OF KOJIRO TOMITA,
for many years Curator of the Asiatic Department
of the Boston Museum of Fine Arts,
who introduced me to Chinese dragon lore.
—M.L.

TO MY TEACHER
Professor Cheng, a painter of all painters.
—E.Y.

THIS SEAL is a Chinese proverb made up of four characters, which, translated literally, mean:
Paint • Dragon • Put • Eye. The proverb is a reference to the legend of the painter Chang Seng
Yung of the state of Wu, who painted four dragons on the walls of Tung-ang temple in Chin Ling
(the present city of Nanking). Two dragons came to life and broke loose when the painter
added their eyes. The other two dragons, who did not receive eyes, remain on the temple walls
to this day.

Text copyright © 1987 by Margaret Leaf.
Illustrations copyright © 1987 by Ed Young.
All rights reserved. No part of this book may be reproduced or
utilized in any form or by any means, electronic or mechanical,
including photocopying, recording or by any information storage
and retrieval system, without permission in writing from the
Publisher. Inquiries should be addressed to Lothrop, Lee & Shepard
Books, a division of William Morrow & Company, Inc., 105
Madison Avenue, New York, New York 10016.
Printed in Hong Kong.

First Edition   5 6 7 8 9 10

Library of Congress Cataloging in Publication Data
Leaf, Margaret.   Eyes of the dragon.
Summary: An artist agrees to paint a dragon on the wall of a
Chinese village, but the magistrate's insistence that he paint eyes
on the dragon has amazing results. [1. Dragons—Fiction. 2. Art-
ists—Fiction. 3. China—Fiction] I. Young, Ed, ill. II. Title.
PZ7.L4628Ey   1987   [E]   85-11670
ISBN 0-688-06155-9   ISBN 0-688-06156-7 (lib. bdg.)

EYES OF THE DRAGON

BY MARGARET LEAF

ILLUSTRATED BY ED YOUNG

LOTHROP, LEE & SHEPARD BOOKS
NEW YORK

L ong ago in faraway China there was a little village. It lay up against a tall mountain on which there lived wild beasts and, some said, wild men. The villagers were afraid.

The village magistrate was worried, and he persuaded the people to build a wall all around the village. When finished, the wall was strong and high, with a gate that could be locked. Over the gate was a little roof, and inside was a screen to keep evil spirits from entering. Everyone now felt safe, and they all slept soundly at night.

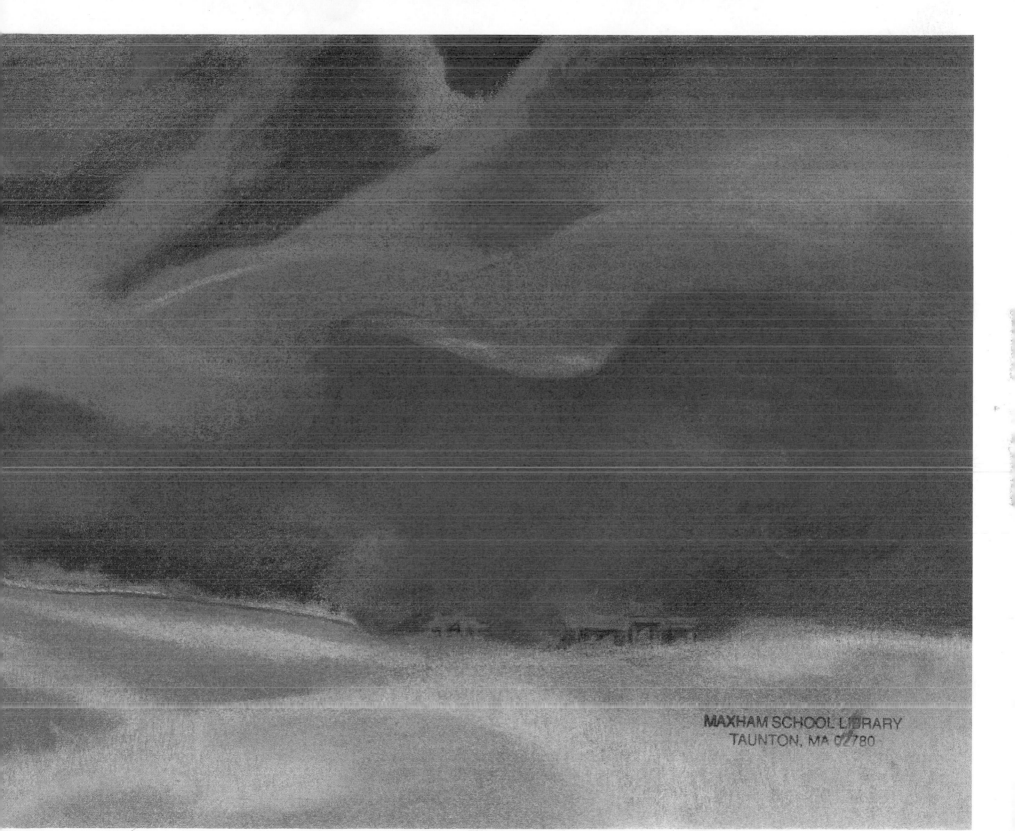

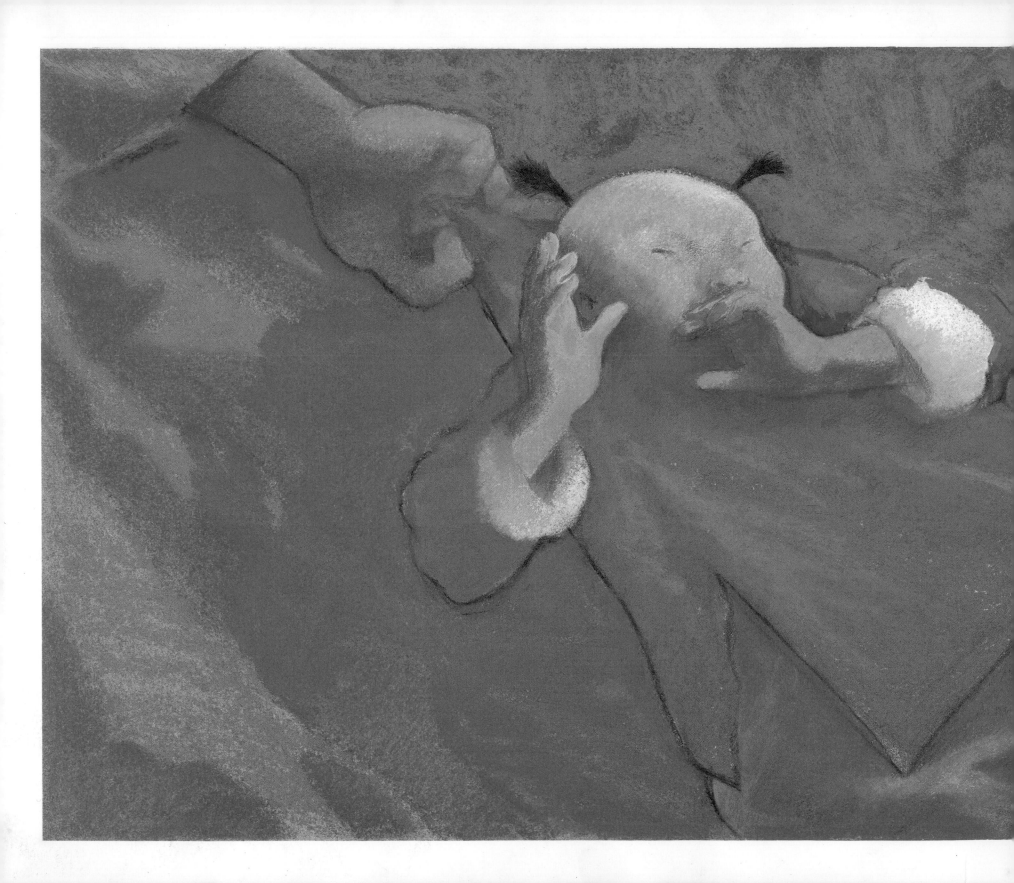

The magistrate, a very proud man, was especially proud of the wall. Every evening after supper he took a walk all around the village, admiring the wall and saying to himself, "How clever I was to think of the wall, and how beautiful it is."

One evening, just as he turned a corner where the wall curved, he saw a group of children clustered around his grandson, Li. He was horrified to see that Li was making marks on the clean surface of the wall.

"Stop!" he shouted at the top of his voice, and the children scattered like a flock of frightened chickens—all but Li, whose collar was firmly held by his grandfather.

"Please, Honorable Grandfather, let me go. We meant no harm. We were just decorating it. It is so plain."

"Very well," his grandfather said sternly. "I won't punish you this time, but be sure never to do it again."

The magistrate, who loved his grandson, let him go and continued his walk, but somehow he felt a bit less satisfied. "Perhaps," he said to himself, "it *is* a little plain."

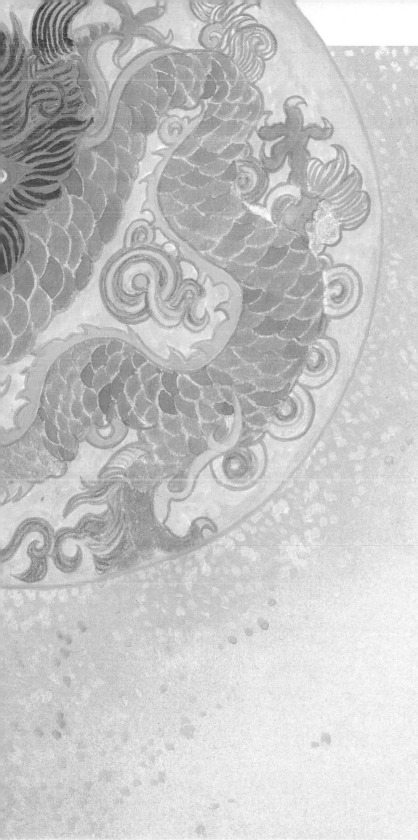

So the next morning he called a meeting of the village elders and spoke to them. "I have been thinking," he said. "Our wall is very strong and protects us well. However, it is a little plain. I have decided we should have it decorated."

They all began to talk at once.

"Maybe the schoolteacher could paint some flowers on it," said one.

"We could cover it with sayings of Confucius," said another.

Then the oldest and wisest of the elders spoke up. "I believe we should have a portrait of the Dragon King painted on our wall. He controls the thunder and lightning and could bring us rain for our fields if he were pleased. You know how dry it has been."

The magistrate nodded his head and said, "Exactly what I have been thinking."

Everybody agreed that this was a good idea. The youngest of the elders, who had been trying to get their attention, said, "Ch'en Jung, the most famous dragon painter, lives in the city. I will gladly go and ask him to come."

It was settled, and the youngest elder set out that same day.

Li watched the road every day after school. On the third day he spied two figures approaching. "Here they come!" he shouted, and the magistrate and elders hurried to the gate. Ch'en Jung was riding a little horse with a big box tied on behind the saddle. The magistrate and elders bowed very politely, and then led Ch'en Jung into the village.

"Now," said the painter, "before I start, you must agree to my conditions. I want your promise that I may paint your dragon in my own manner and that you will accept it. You must also give me forty silver coins, which I will donate to followers of the Tao who are building a temple in the city."

The magistrate spoke for them all and promised. Ch'en Jung then opened his box, put together a little table for his paints and brushes, and started to work. He began on the left side of the gate, carefully drawing the dragon's tail.

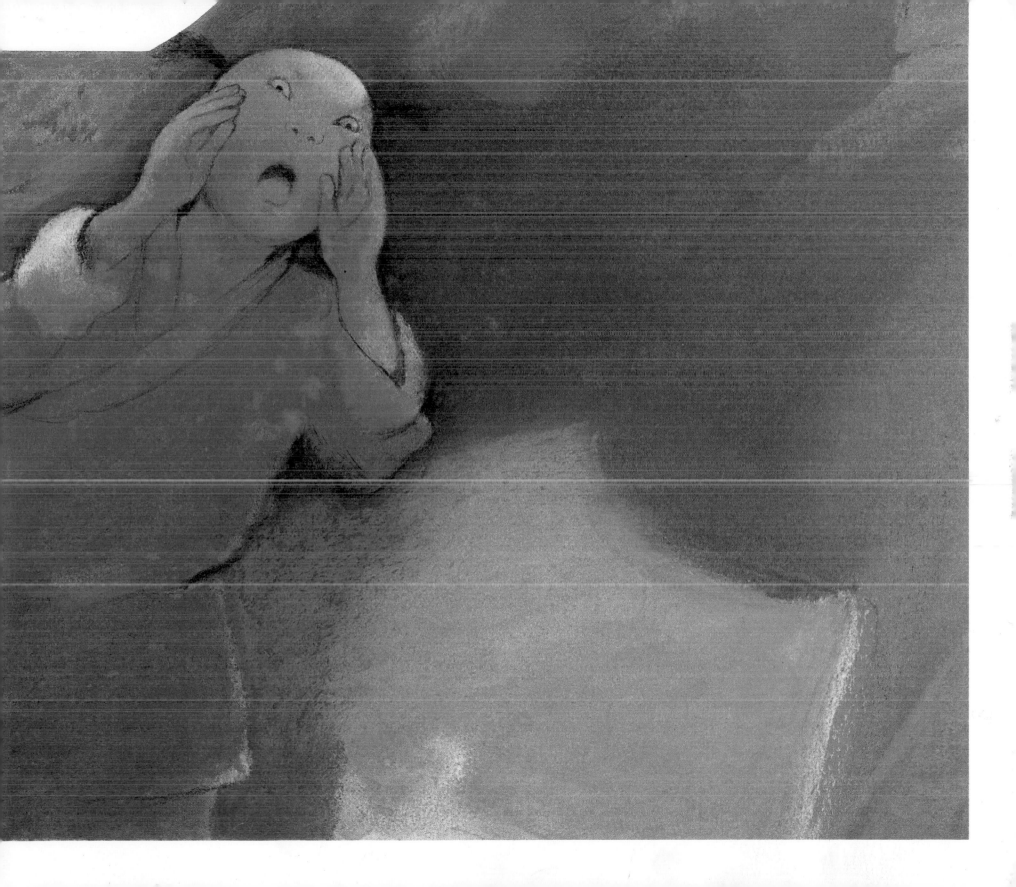

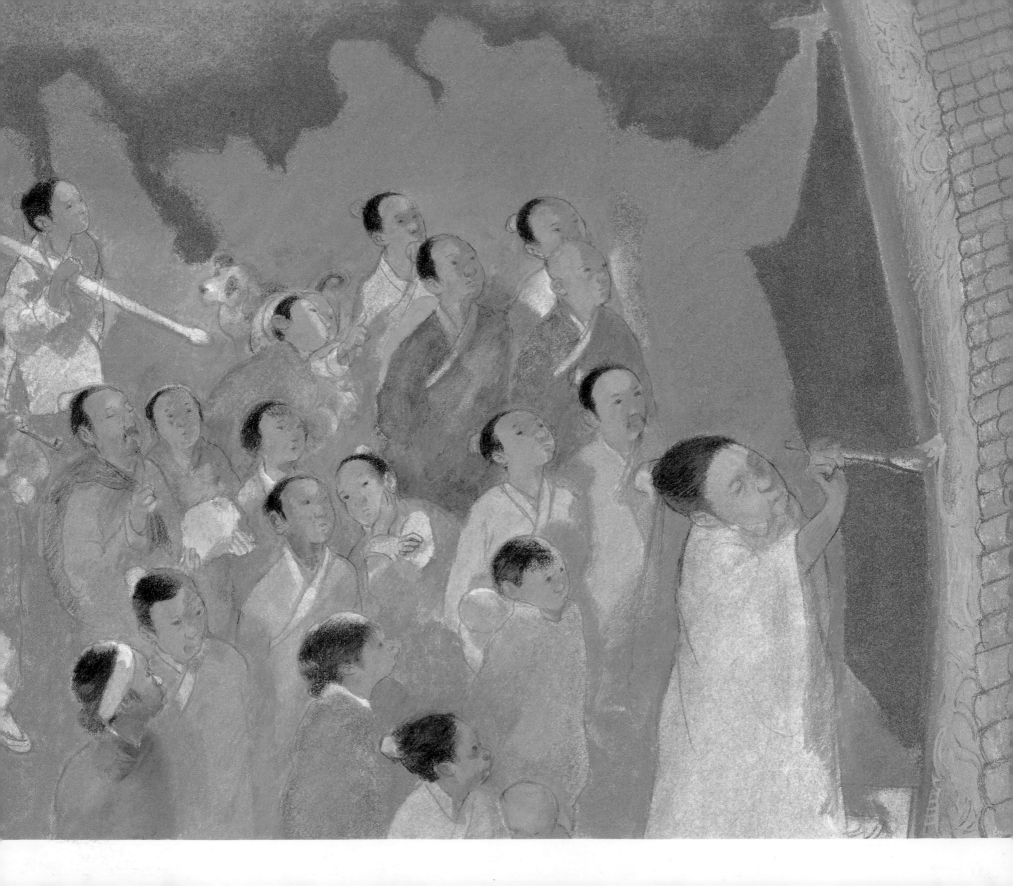

Everyone watched. The children on their way to school walked so slowly that they were late and had to stay after their lessons. The women on their way to market took so long to get there that dinners were late. The old men just sat all day with their backs to the houses and watched. The men who worked all day in the fields inspected the progress each night after supper. And the magistrate, of course, watched all day, looking very important.

Ch'en Jung painted steadily, and little by little the long body of the dragon appeared on the wall. Finally the painter reached the right side of the gate, and the dragon's head met his tail. The painting was magnificent.

"Yes," said Ch'en Jung. "The Heavenly King will be pleased. I have finished."

He packed his paints and table back into the box and called for his little horse. He then turned to the elders and said, "I am ready to return to the city. I will accept your donation to the Taoist temple now."

"Forty silver coins is no small gift, Ch'en Jung," said the magistrate. "We must first look at your dragon to make certain he is as he should be."

Ch'en Jung gave his consent to an inspection. Starting at the tail, he led the magistrate and elders around the wall. Li and his friends followed as closely as they could. "After all," whispered Li, "decorating the wall was really our idea." Then came the rest of the villagers.

The dragon's body was covered with fiery red scales like those of a fish. The magistrate counted carefully to be sure there were just eighty-one in each row. Li, who was right behind him, counted on his abacus. "This is important," he reminded his friends. "Nine is a lucky number, and nine times nine is eighty-one." The fins on the end of the tail looked so real that Li was afraid to get close.

"You will notice the feet on each of the four legs," said Ch'en Jung. "They have the paws of a tiger and the claws of a hawk. Of course your dragon has four claws on each foot. Only the Emperor's dragon may have five."

As they walked, the dragon's body got bigger and bigger. The scales along his back looked like a row of mountains. Finally they arrived at the great head shaped like a camel's, with heavy shaggy eyebrows, the horns of a deer, the ears of an ox, sharp tusks in the mouth, and a pointed beard with long streaming bristles. Under his chin a large pearl glistened with all the colors of the rainbow. The dragon was so grand and beautiful that no one made a sound. They just stood and looked.

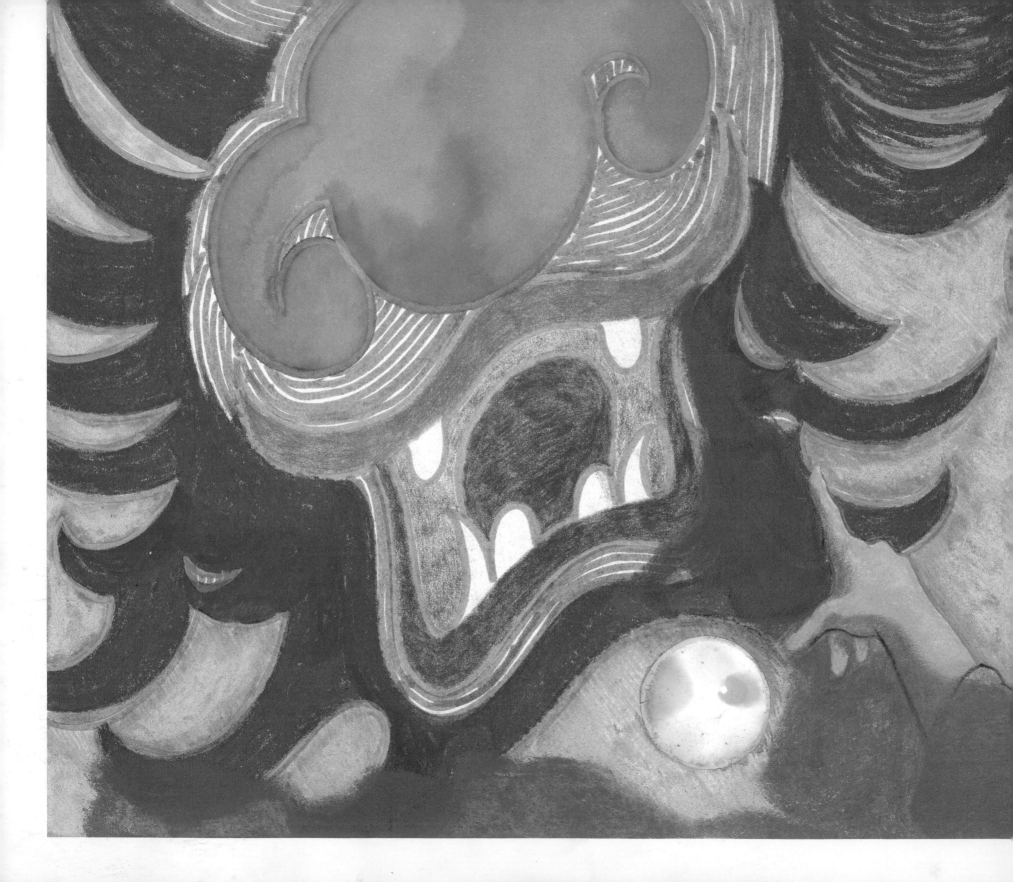

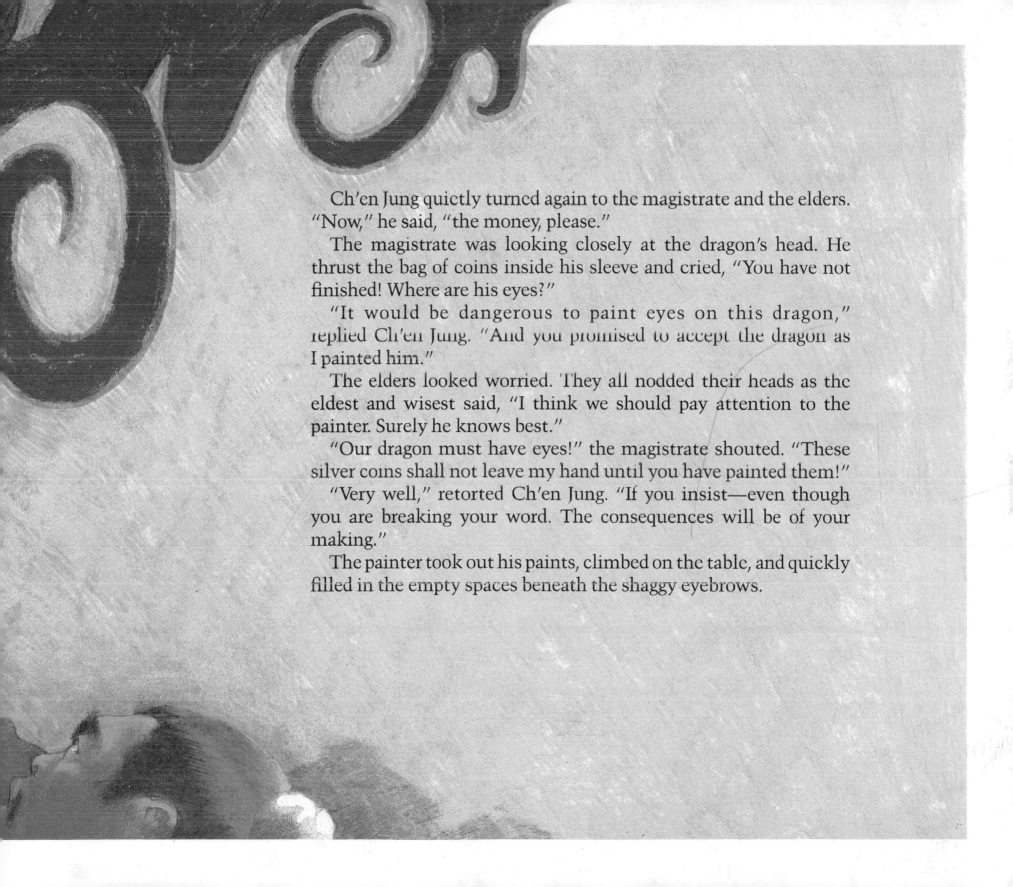

Ch'en Jung quietly turned again to the magistrate and the elders. "Now," he said, "the money, please."

The magistrate was looking closely at the dragon's head. He thrust the bag of coins inside his sleeve and cried, "You have not finished! Where are his eyes?"

"It would be dangerous to paint eyes on this dragon," replied Ch'en Jung. "And you promised to accept the dragon as I painted him."

The elders looked worried. They all nodded their heads as the eldest and wisest said, "I think we should pay attention to the painter. Surely he knows best."

"Our dragon must have eyes!" the magistrate shouted. "These silver coins shall not leave my hand until you have painted them!"

"Very well," retorted Ch'en Jung. "If you insist—even though you are breaking your word. The consequences will be of your making."

The painter took out his paints, climbed on the table, and quickly filled in the empty spaces beneath the shaggy eyebrows.

Ch'en Jung stepped down from the table, took the bag of coins
from the magistrate, packed up, and left.

While the villagers stood
and admired the dragon, the
newly painted eyes seemed to glow
more and more brightly, as though there
were fire within. A wisp of smoke curled up
from the wide-open nostrils and the scales began
to glisten. The air was still, and in the west a great
black cloud climbed the sky and the wind began to blow.

A little boy cried, "He wiggled!" and hid behind his mother.
The people drew back. Li moved closer to his grandfather.

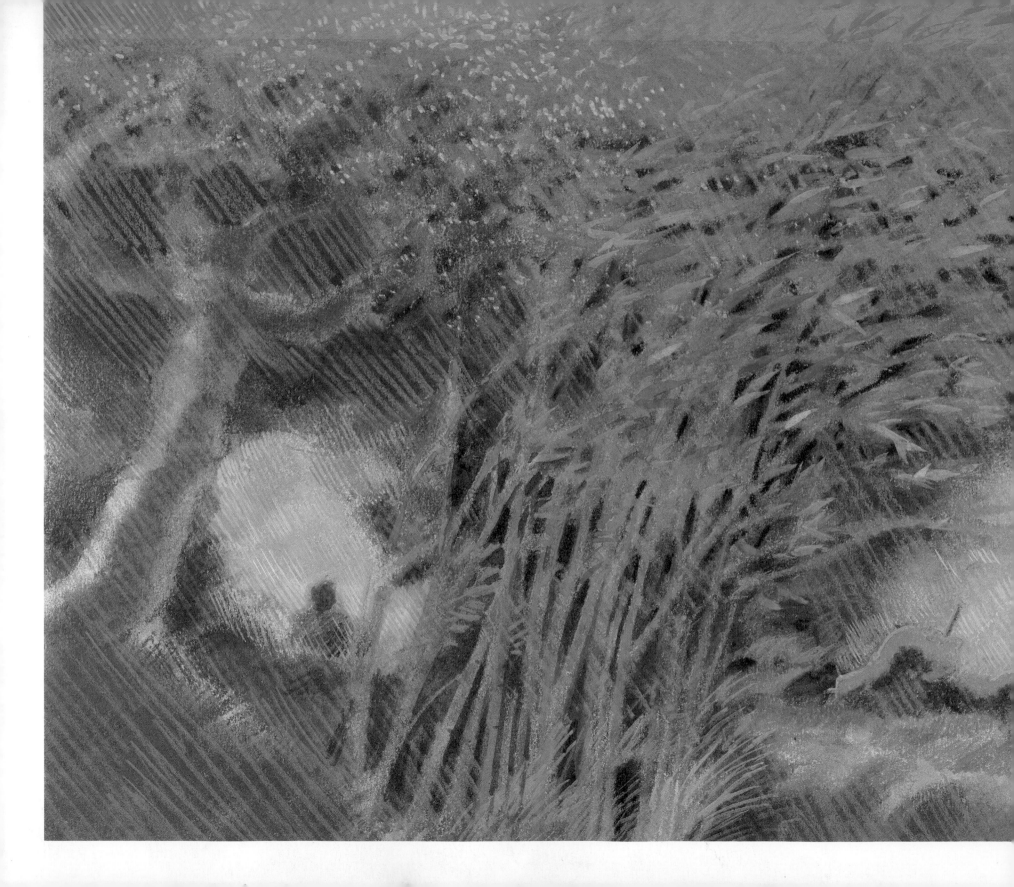

Suddenly the dragon shook himself, and little cracks appeared in the wall. The heavens became dark. The big black cloud moved overhead, there was a loud clap of thunder, and lightning zigzagged across the sky. The dragon shook himself again and—with a scream that sounded like the striking together of two copper vessels—rose into the air and disappeared into the black cloud. The wall crumbled and fell in pieces on the ground.

Down the road a figure on a little horse, with a big box strapped on behind, could be seen hurrying toward the city.

EDITOR'S NOTE ABOUT EYES OF THE DRAGON

Margaret Leaf first became fascinated with the dragon in Chinese culture and art in the early 1960s, when she was working at the Boston Museum of Fine Arts. There she was introduced to the Nine Dragons handscroll, which was painted by the thirteenth-century artist Ch'en Jung. She never forgot Ch'en Jung, about whom a contemporary, on seeing the Nine Dragons, wrote, "Could it be that he holds a gift from Heaven in his bosom?" His life and work as an itinerant dragon painter were the inspiration for this story about a little boy whose prideful grandfather placed having his own way ahead of honoring his word.

The harmonious principles of dragon-painting are defined in an ancient essay ascribed by some to the Ming painter T'ang Yin. The essay offers a philosophical approach to the dragon painter's task: "Dragon-painting should be in accordance with the Way of the Spirit and the Life-breath. The Spirit is like the mother, and the Life-breath is like the child. When the Spirit summons the Life-breath as the mother summons the child, how would it dare not to come? Consequently, dragons should rise to heaven through dense mist and layers of clouds, or immerse themselves in the bottomless depths of turbulent waters where no human eye can reach them."

The essay goes on to declare, "You must paint with a sweeping brush . . . so as to bring out the life of the muscles and the bones, but in order to express the essence of the spirit of the dragon perfectly, you must give him awe-inspiring, bloody eyes . . . then, when the eyes are put in, he will fly away."

Ed Young's masterful use of pastels to interpret Margaret Leaf's story is in keeping with the methods of the dragon painters of old. He has abided by the instruction to reach for the idea of cosmic transformations, and has filled his paintings with an energy that is at once of this world, and yet from another.

Illustrations executed in pastels on Arches paper • Designed by Cindy Simon •
Composed by Expertype, Inc., on a Linotron 202 Mergenthaler in Trump Medieval with display lines in Trump Medieval Bold •
Title calligraphy by John Stevens • Color separations by South China Printing Co., Hong Kong •
Printed on 128 GSM Matte paper and bound by South China Printing Co.

E
LEA

Leaf, Margaret

Eyes of the dragon

$16.93